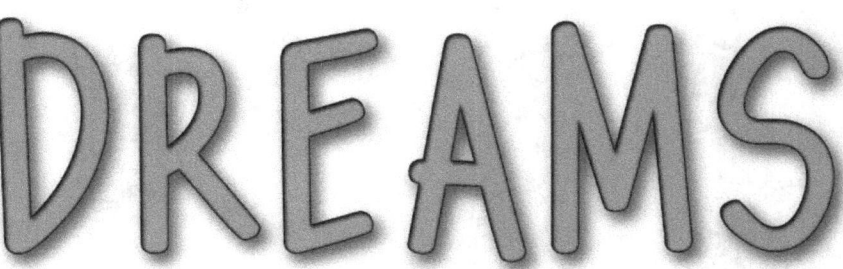

DREAMS

first anti-stress coloring book
by ARIMI

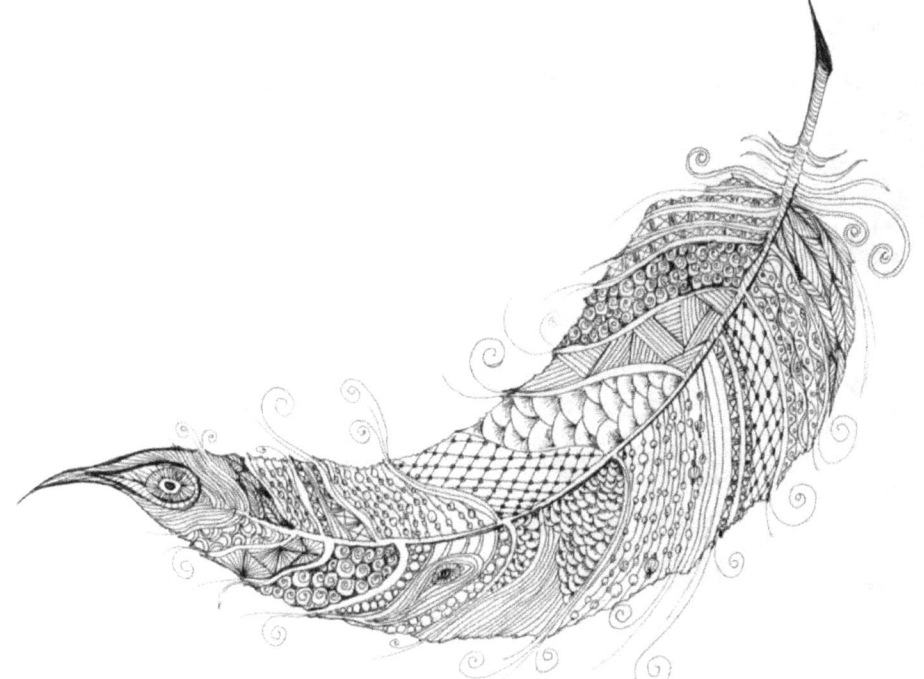

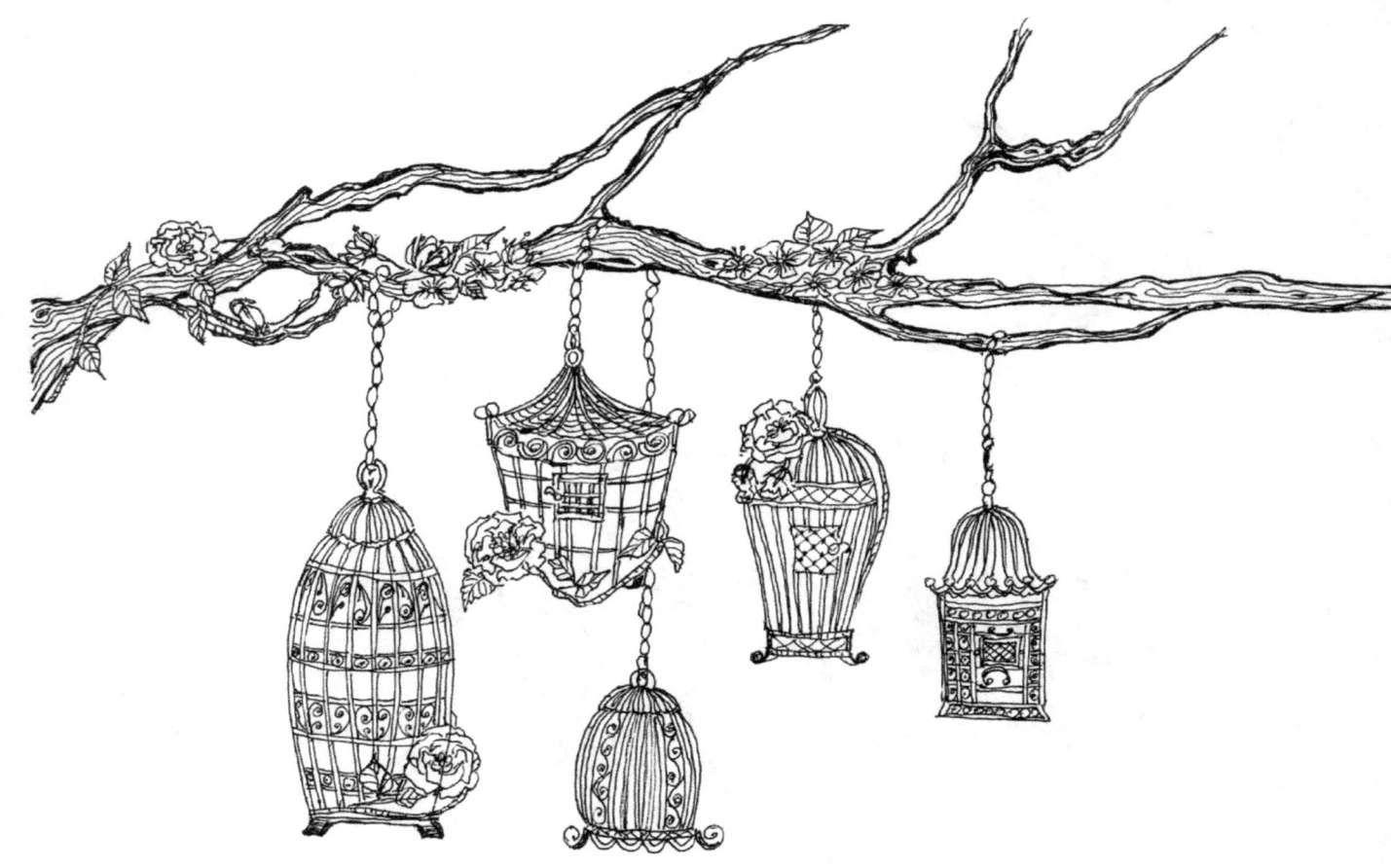

Where the spirit does not work with the hand there is no art
Leonardo da Vinci

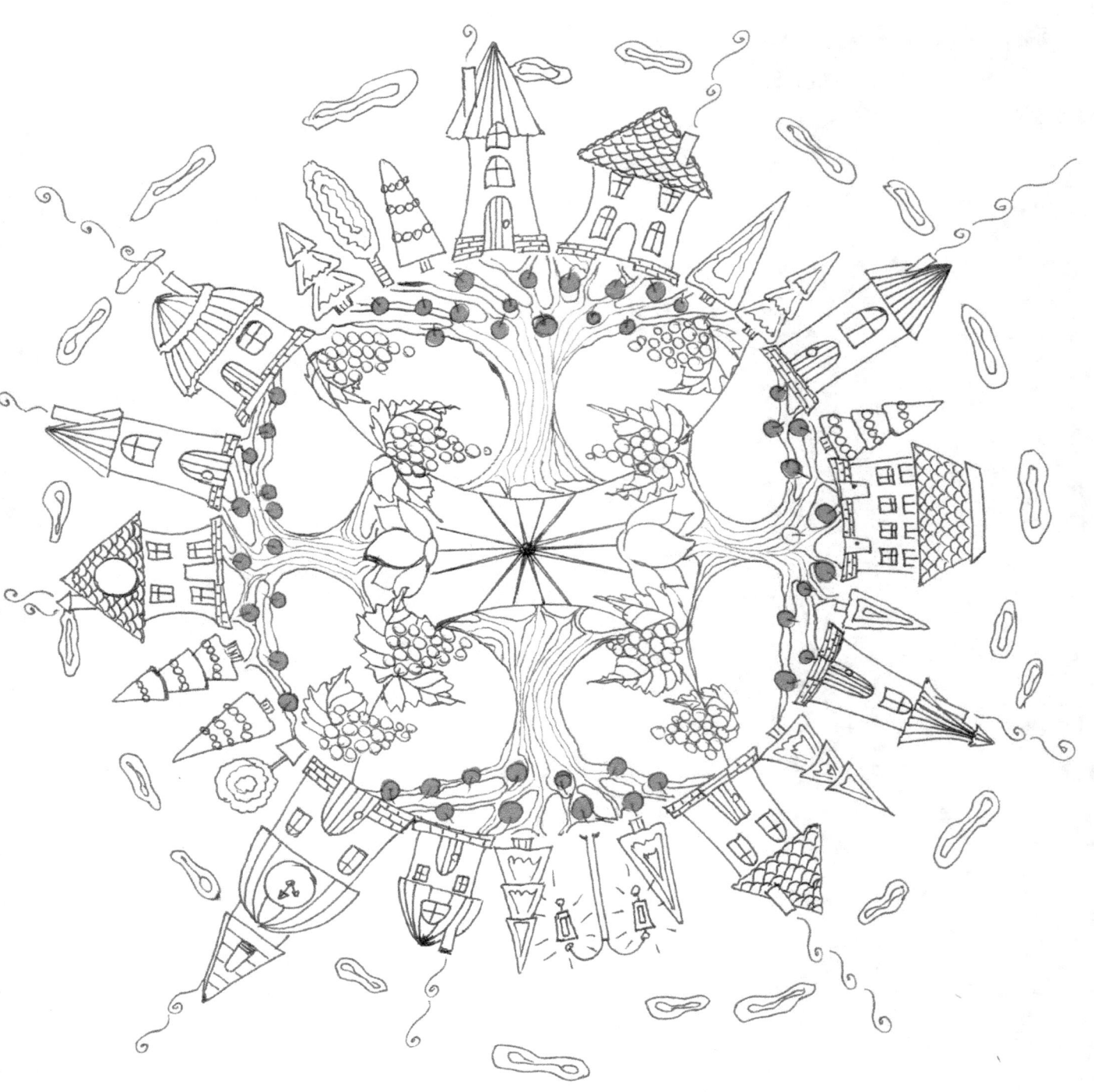

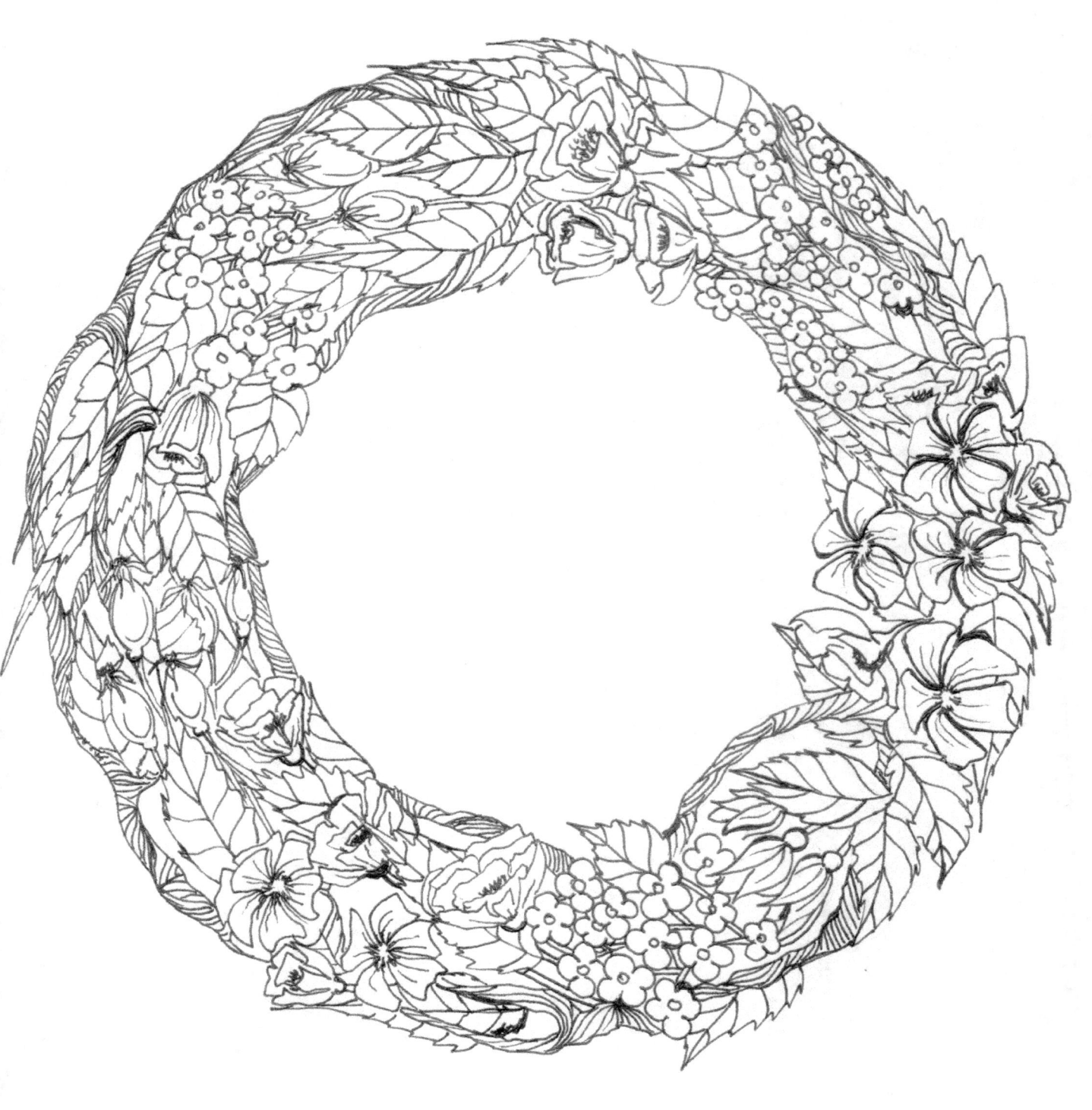

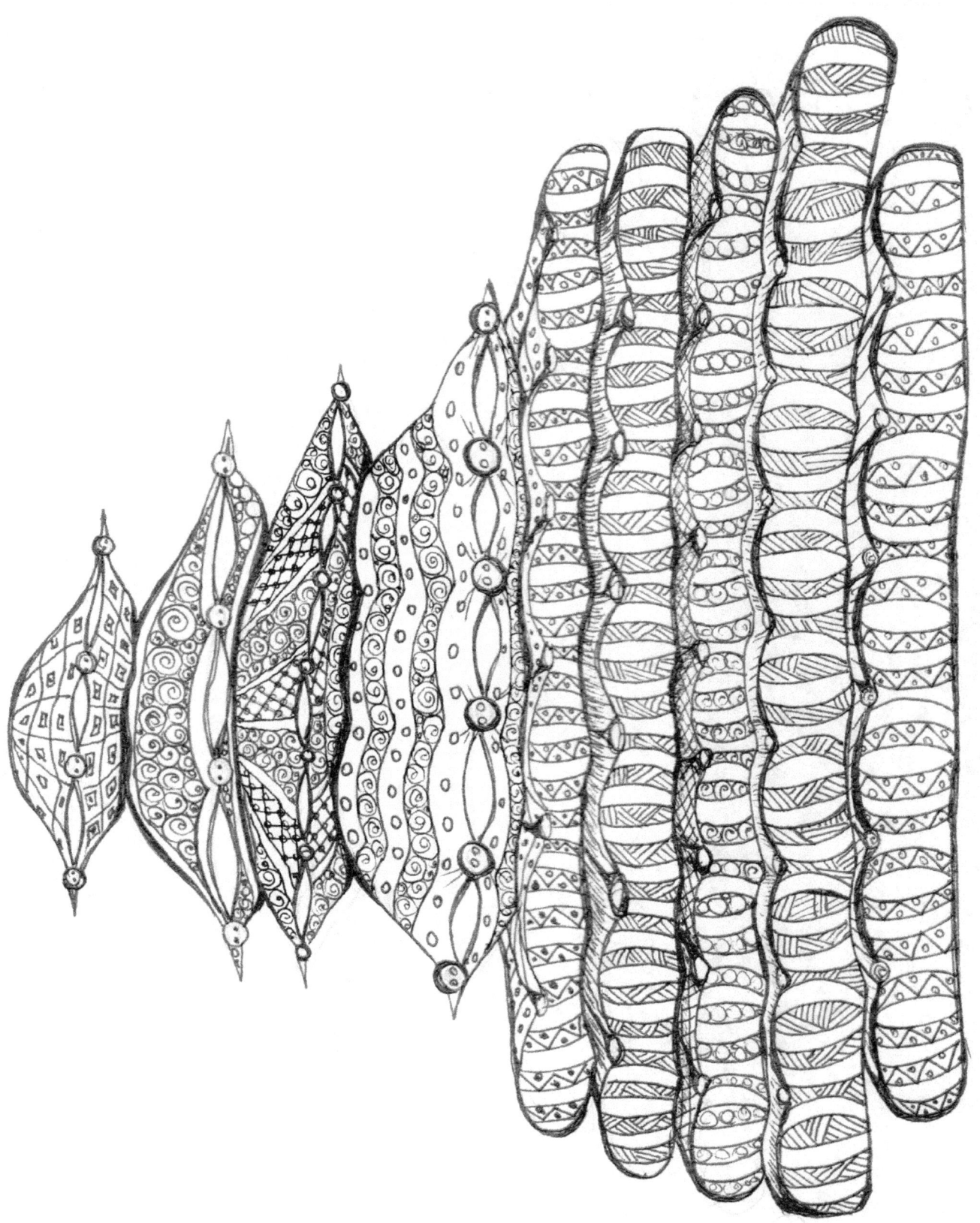

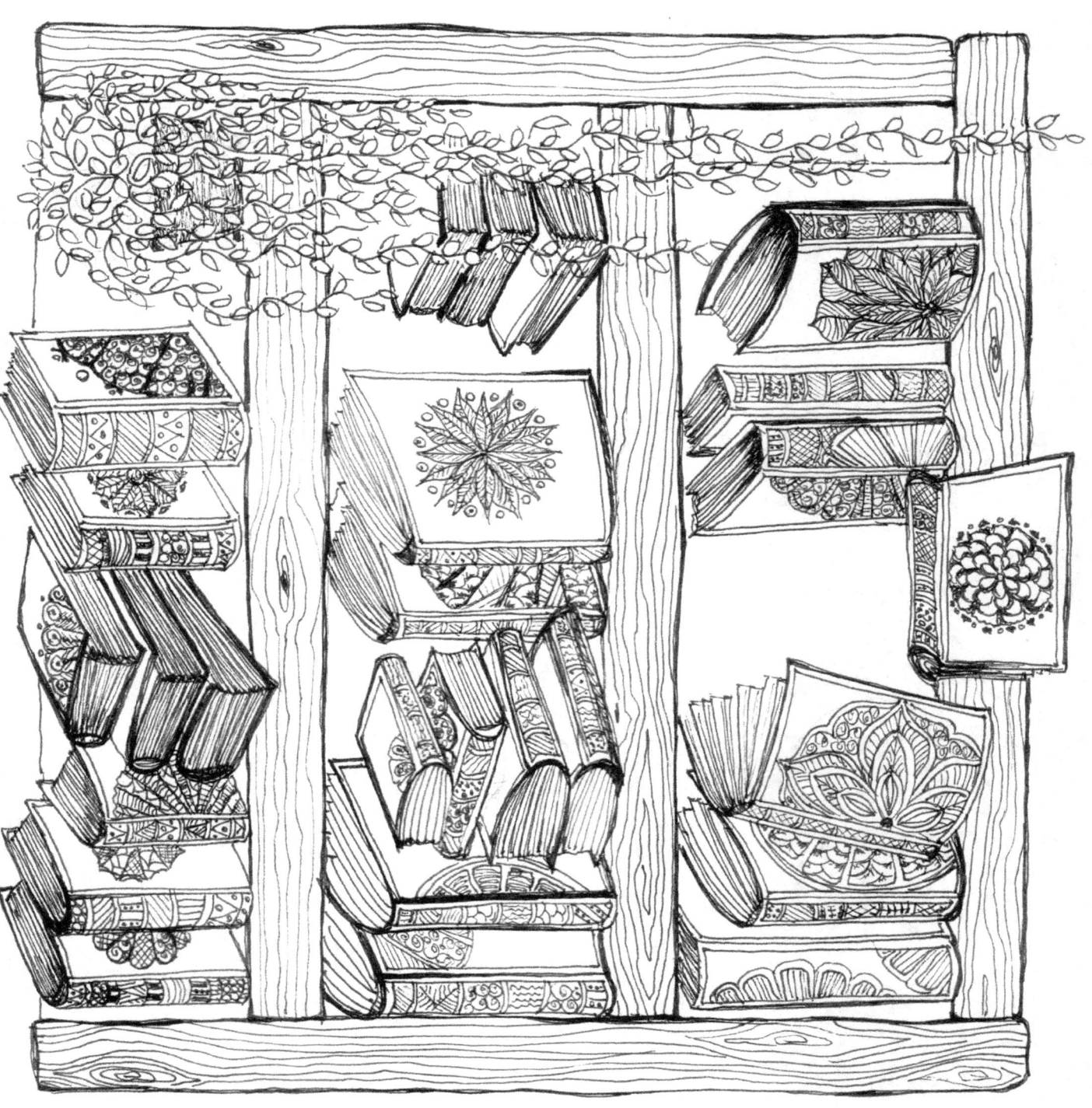

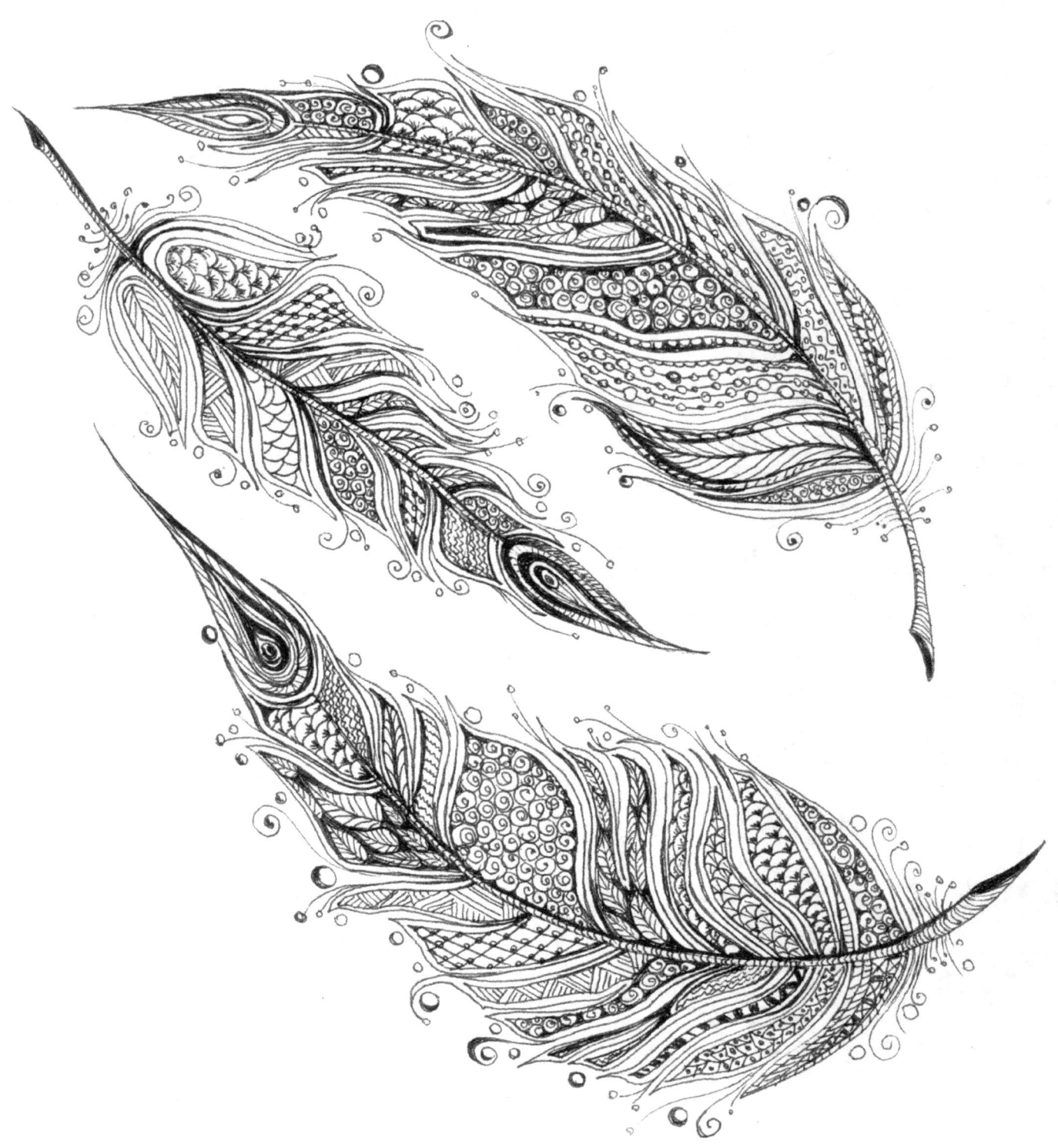

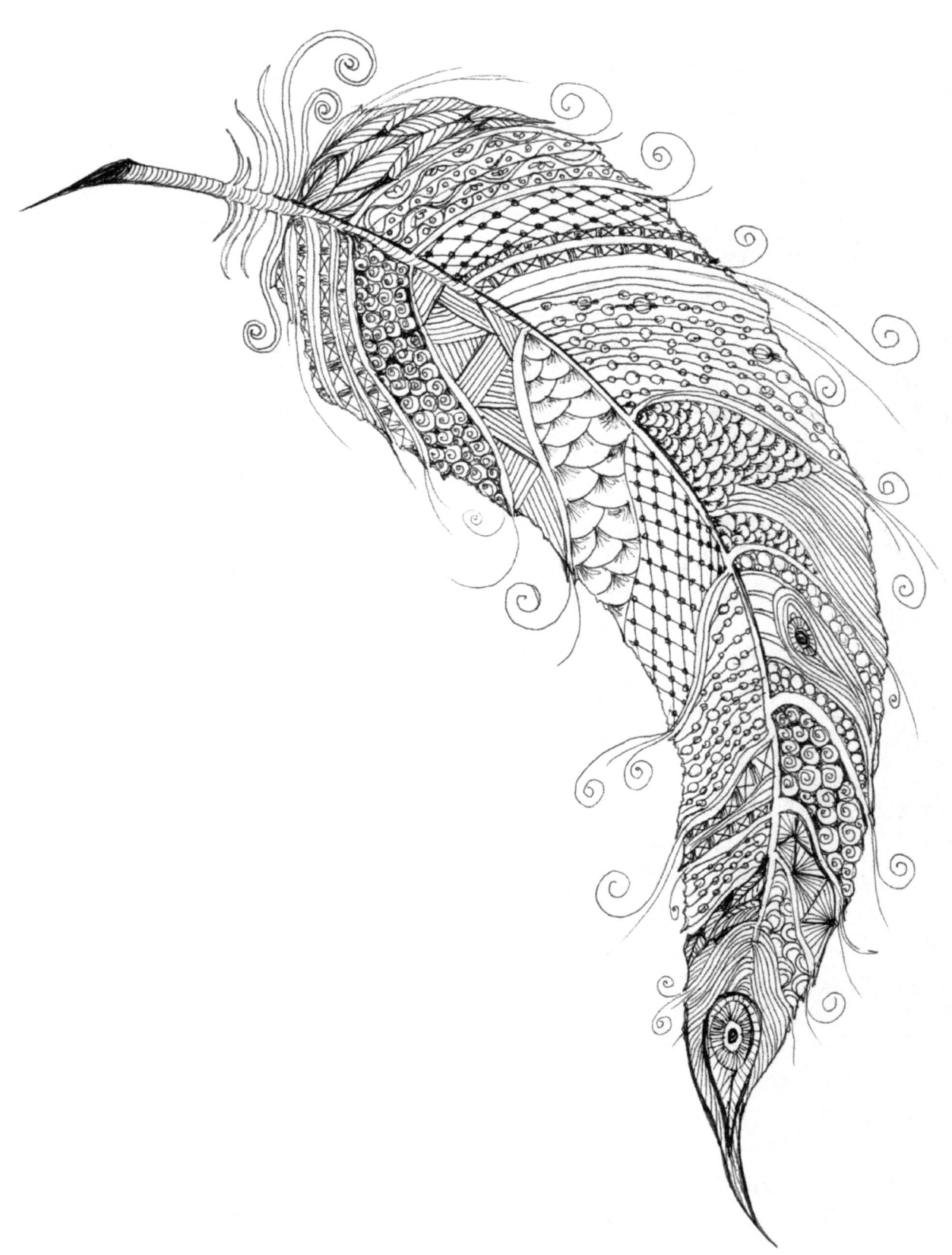

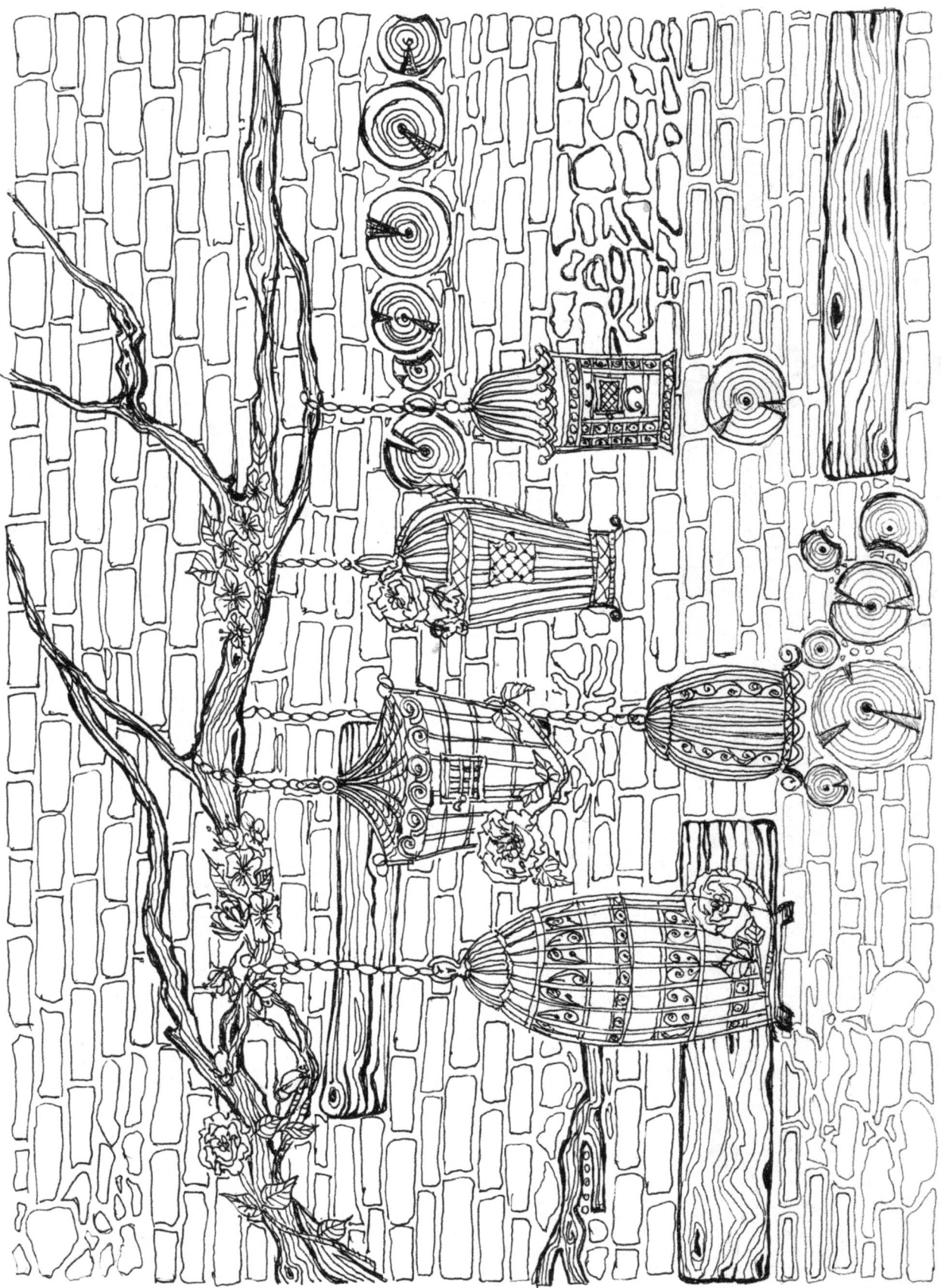

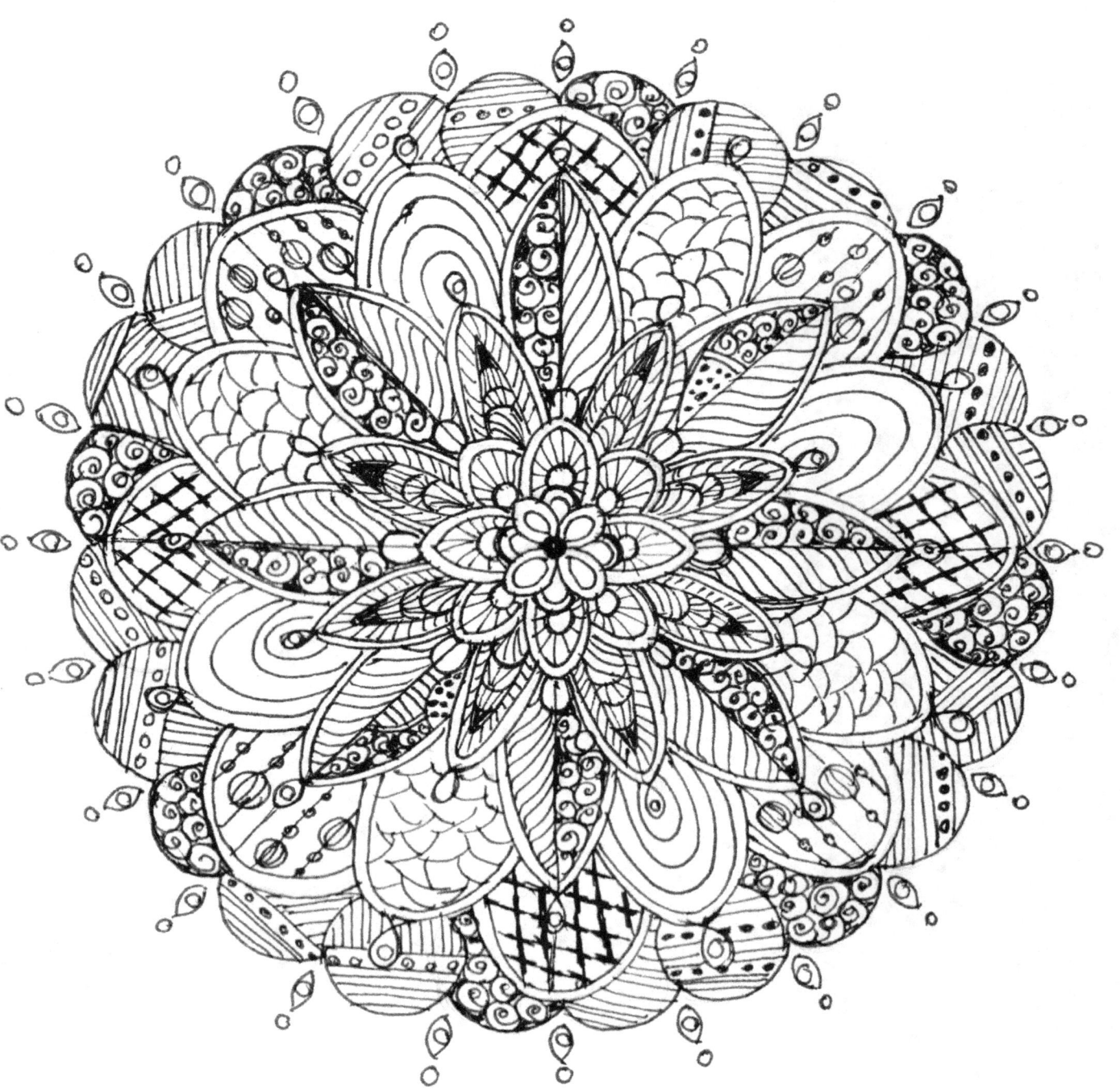

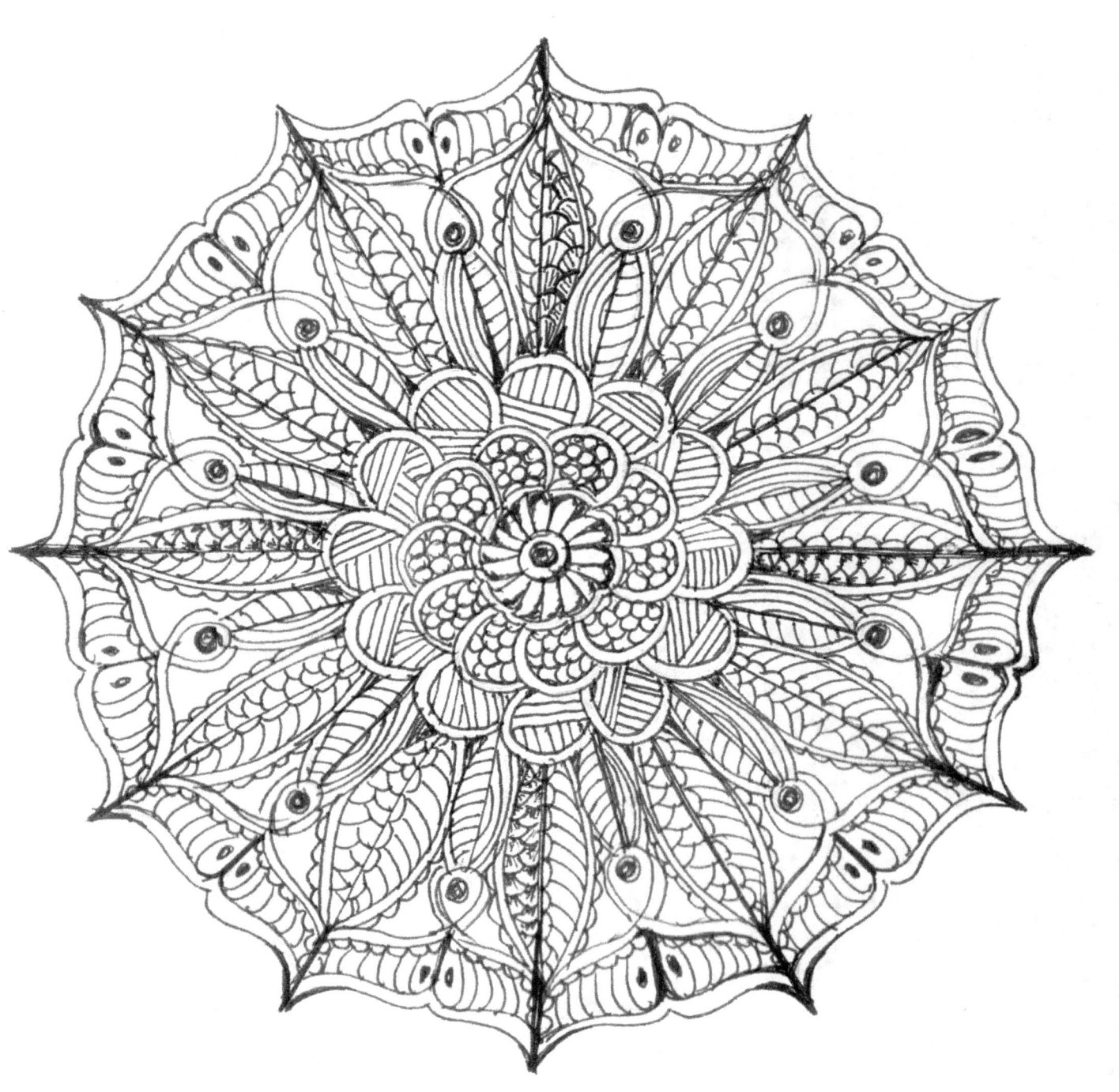

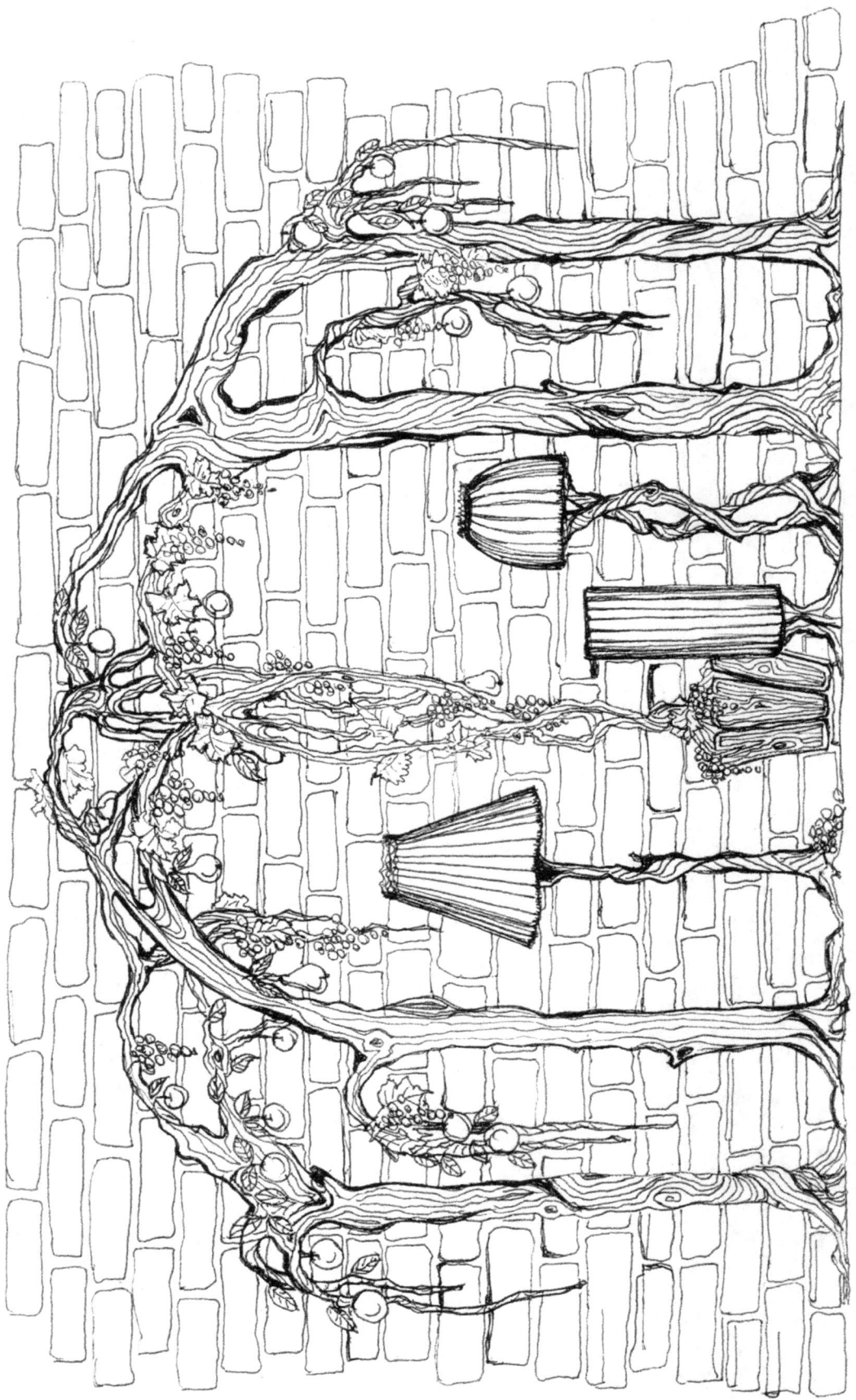

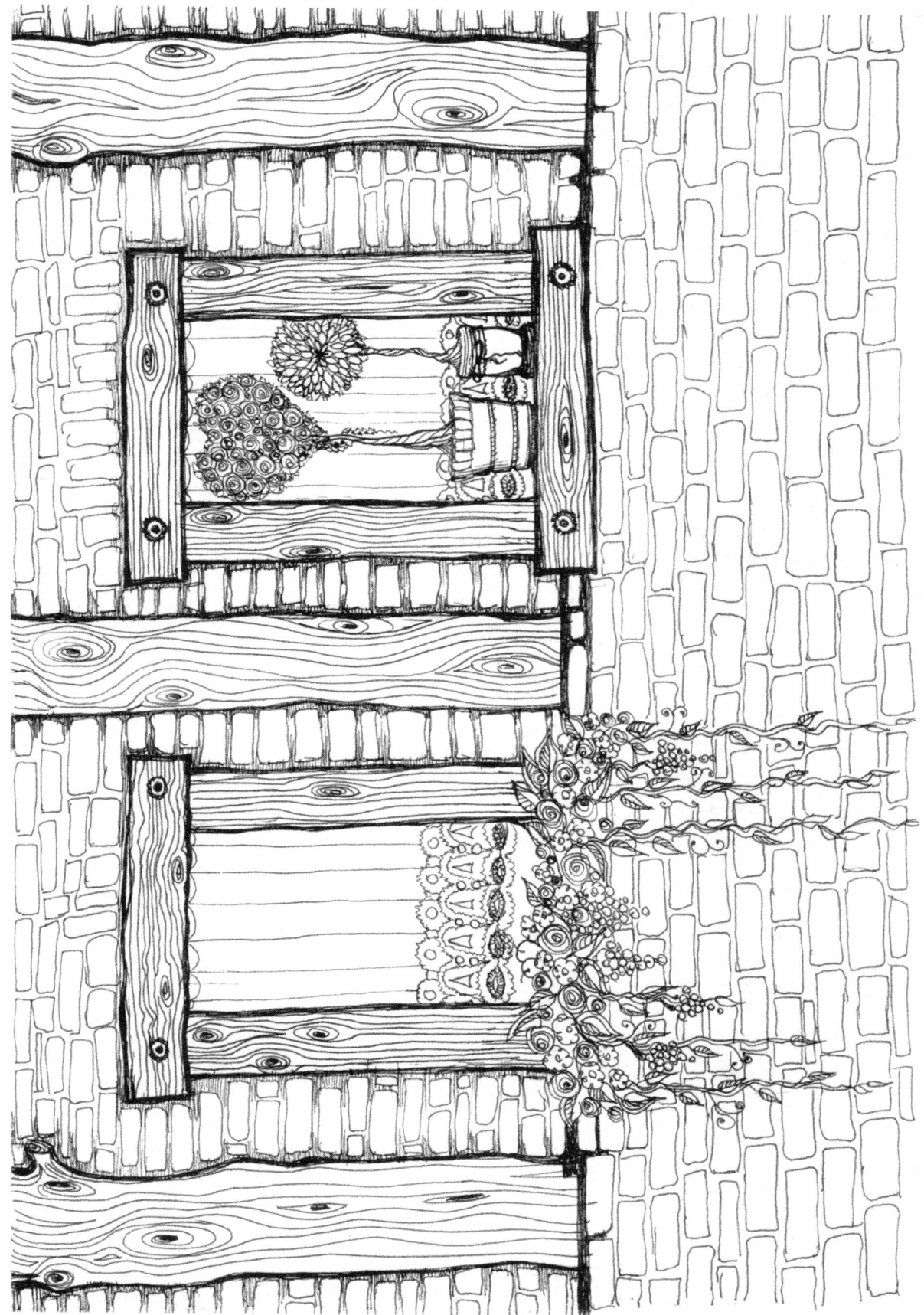

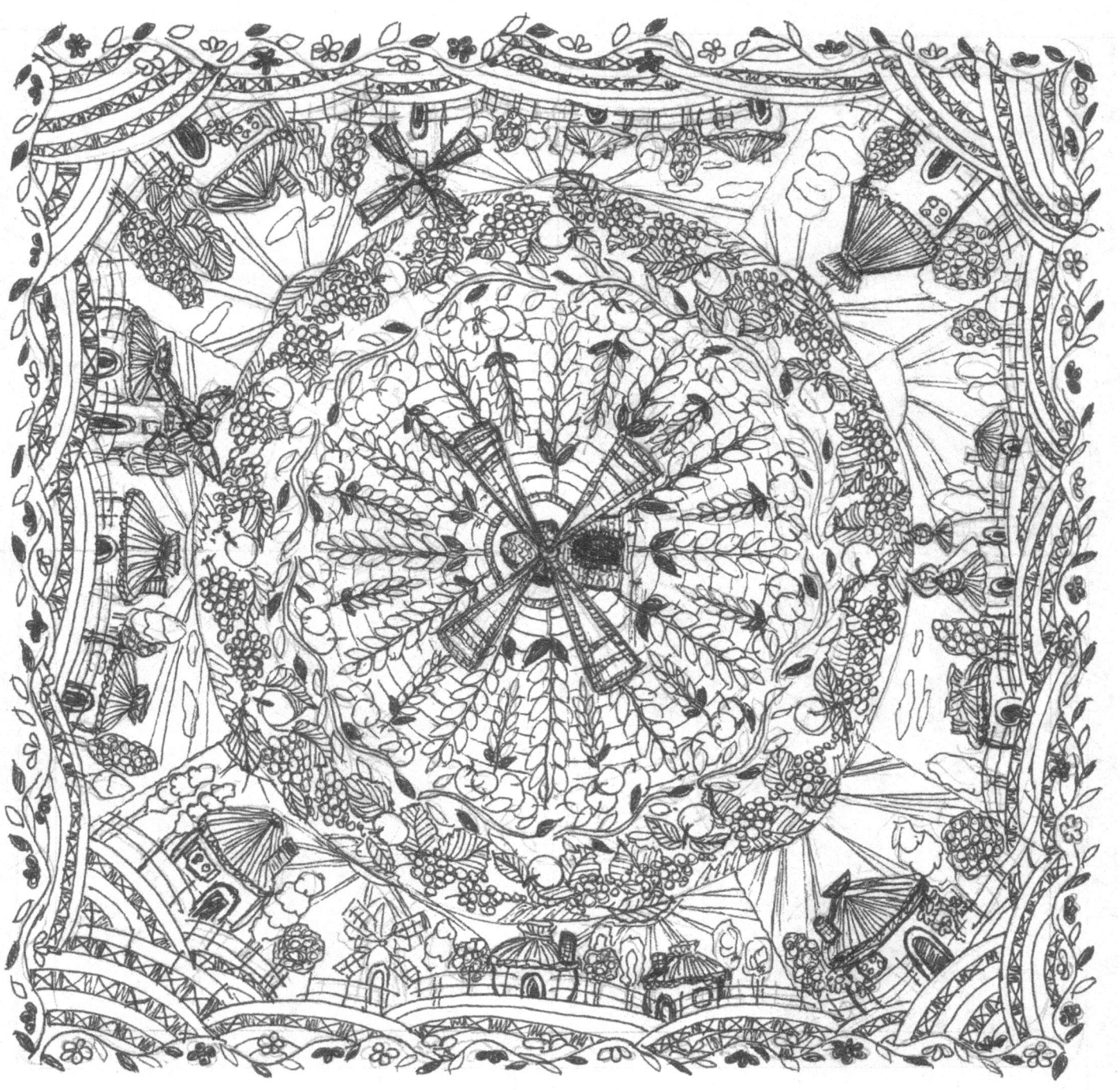

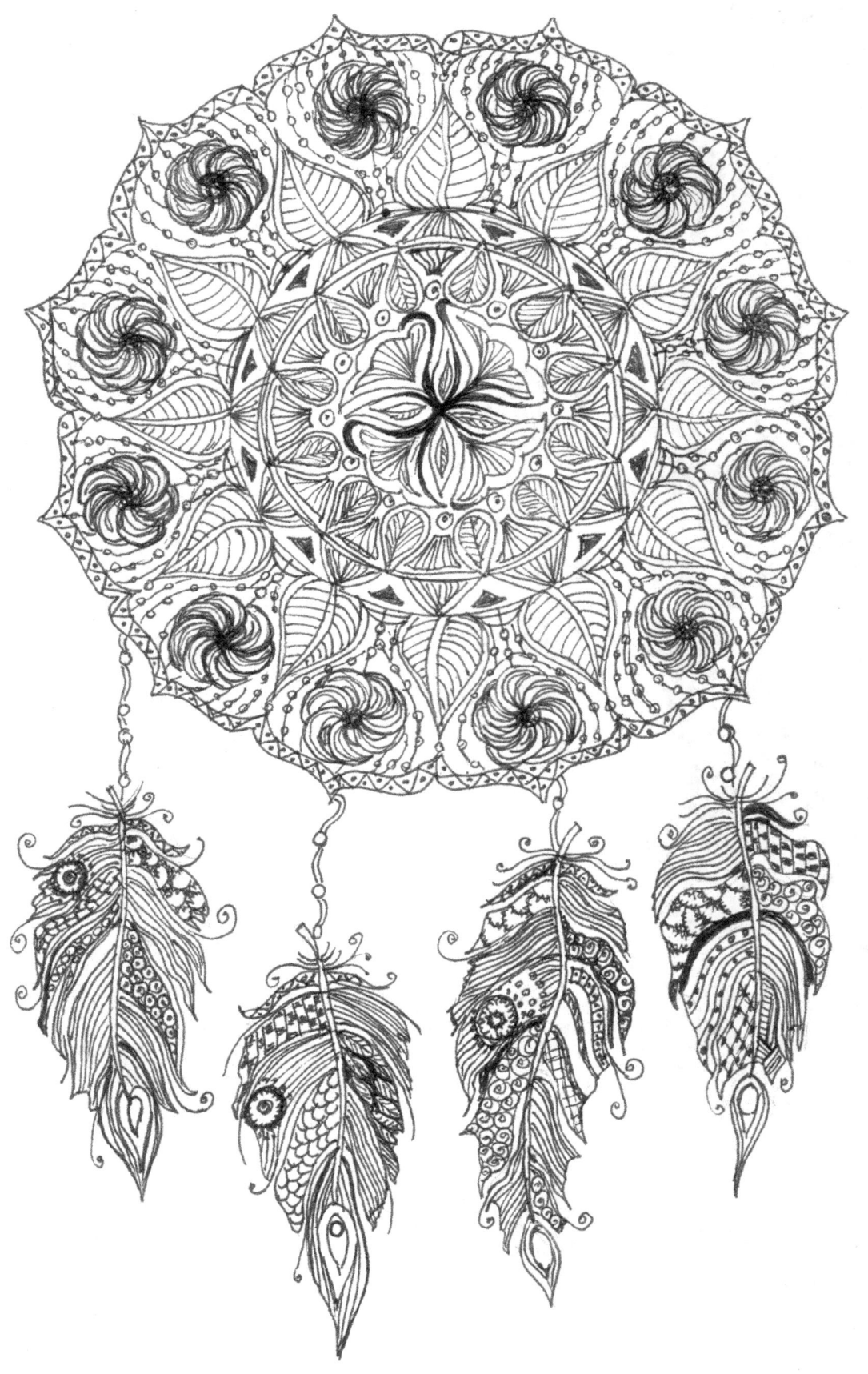

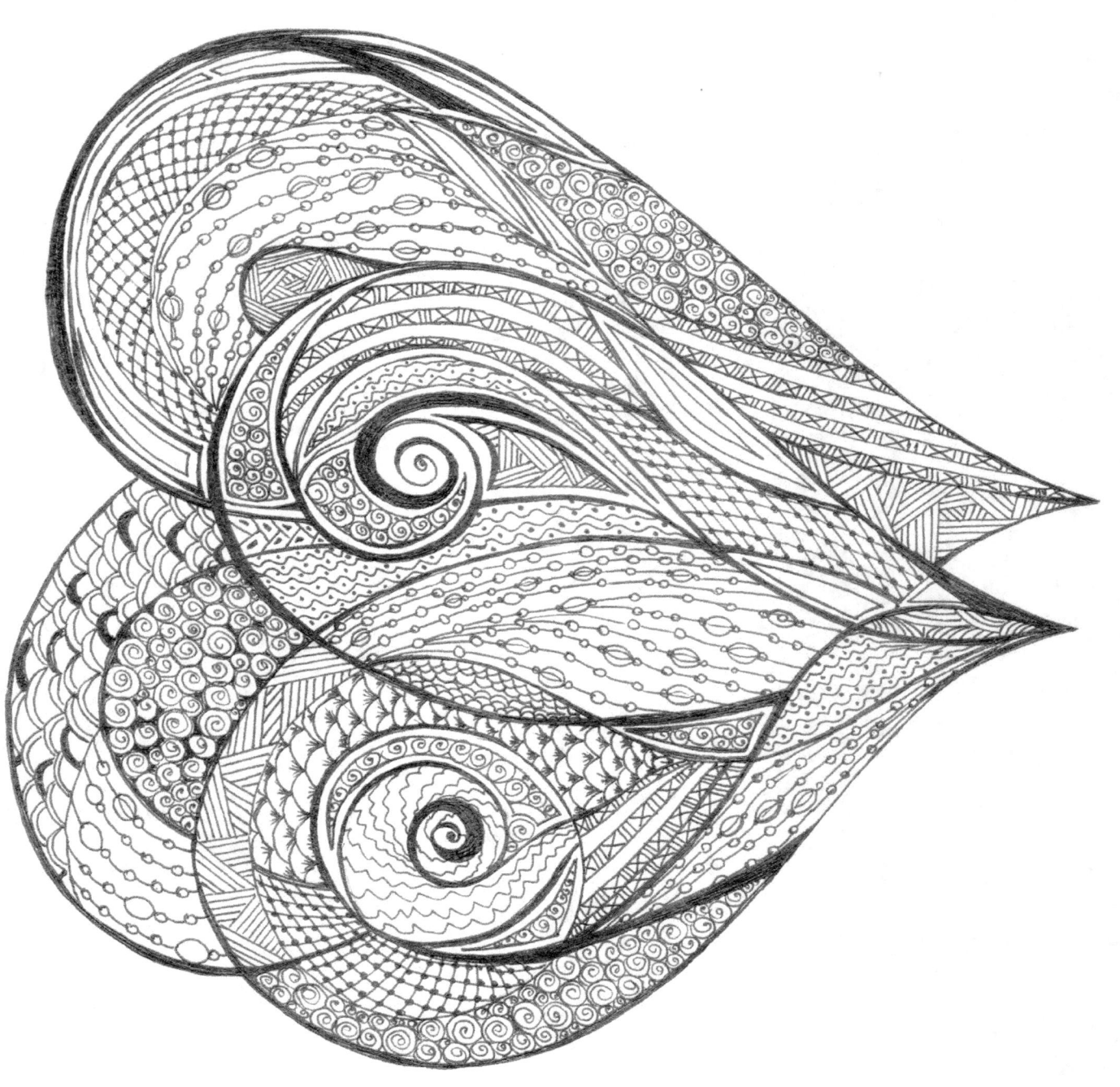

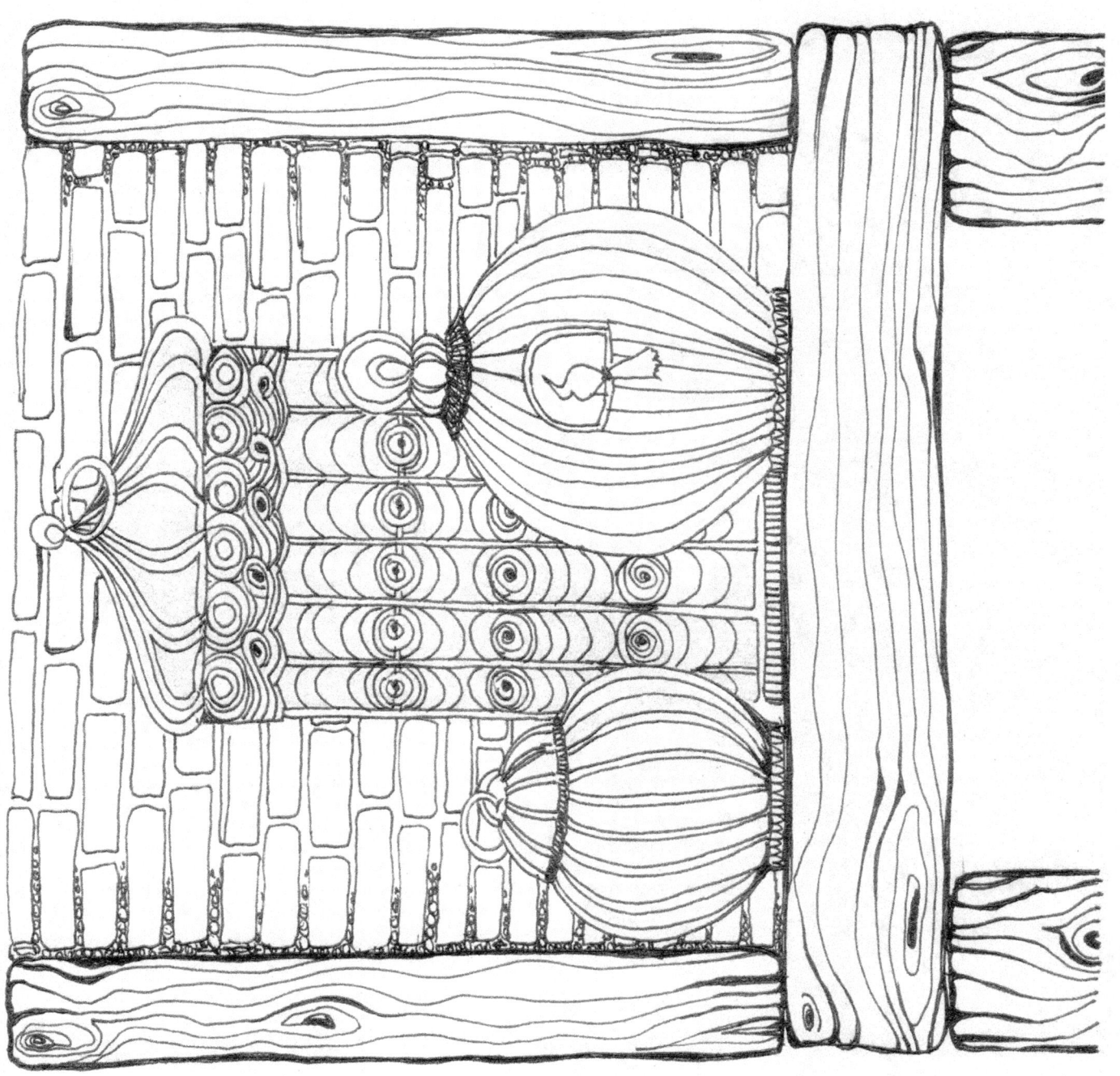

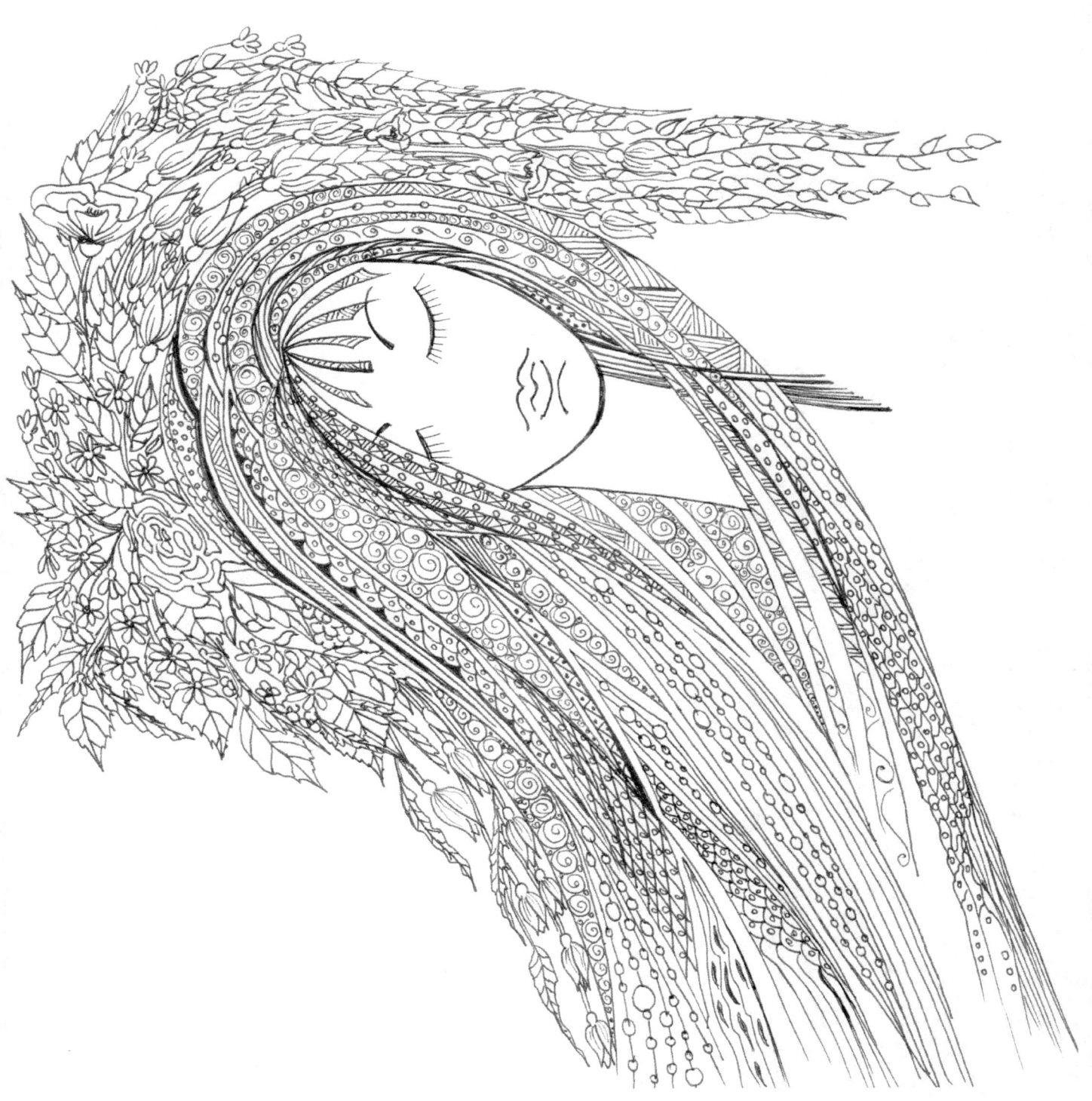

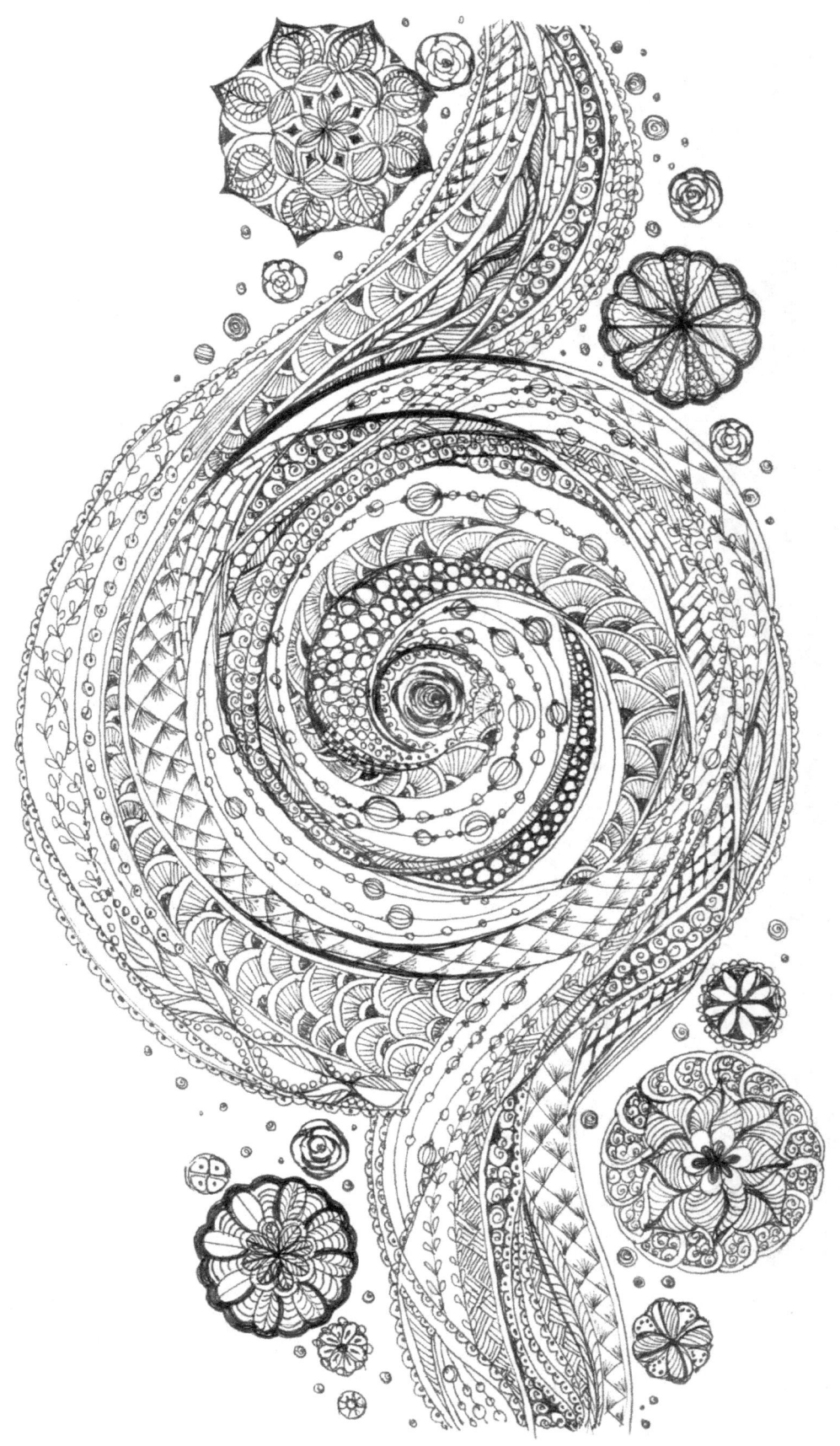

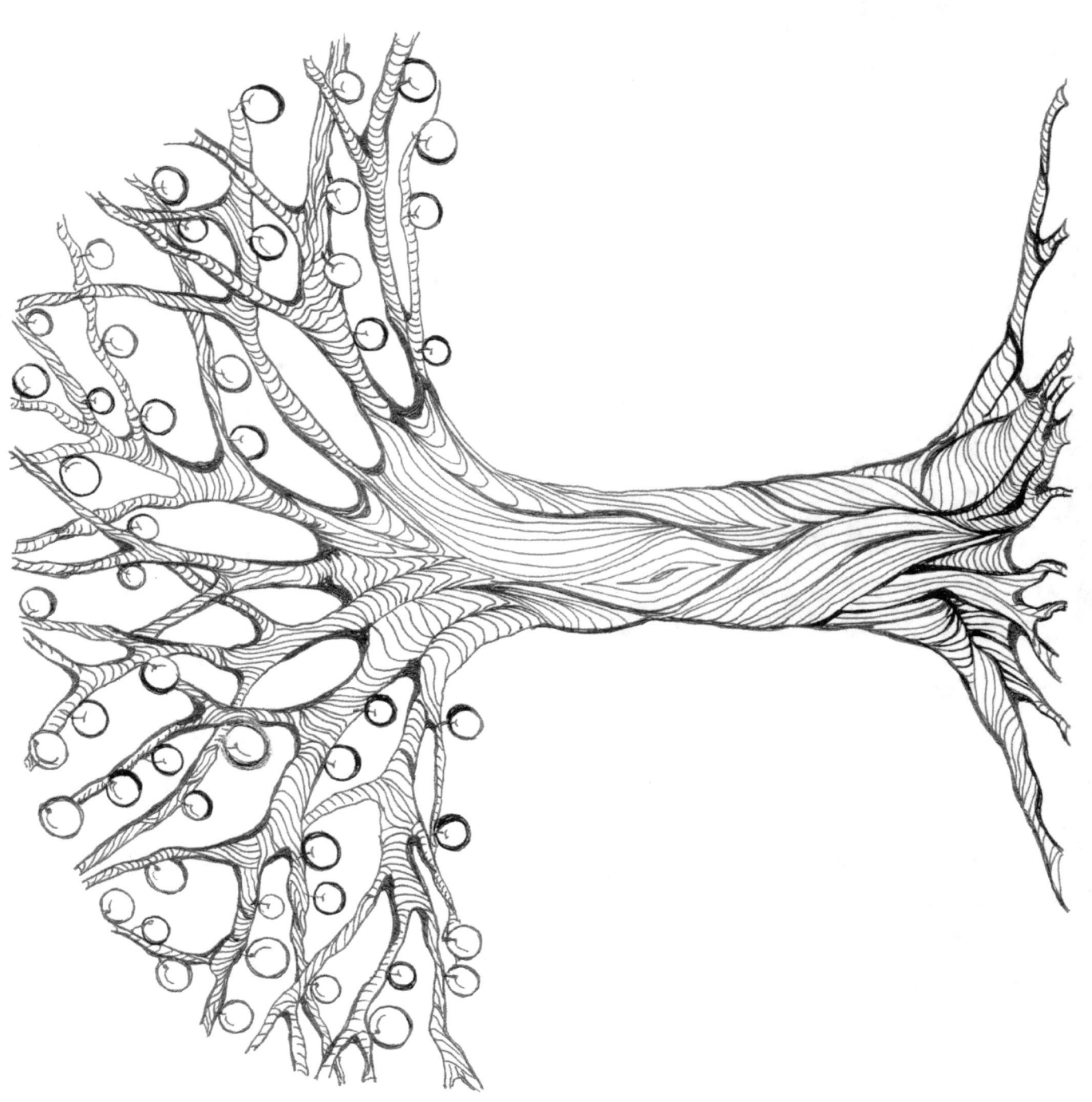

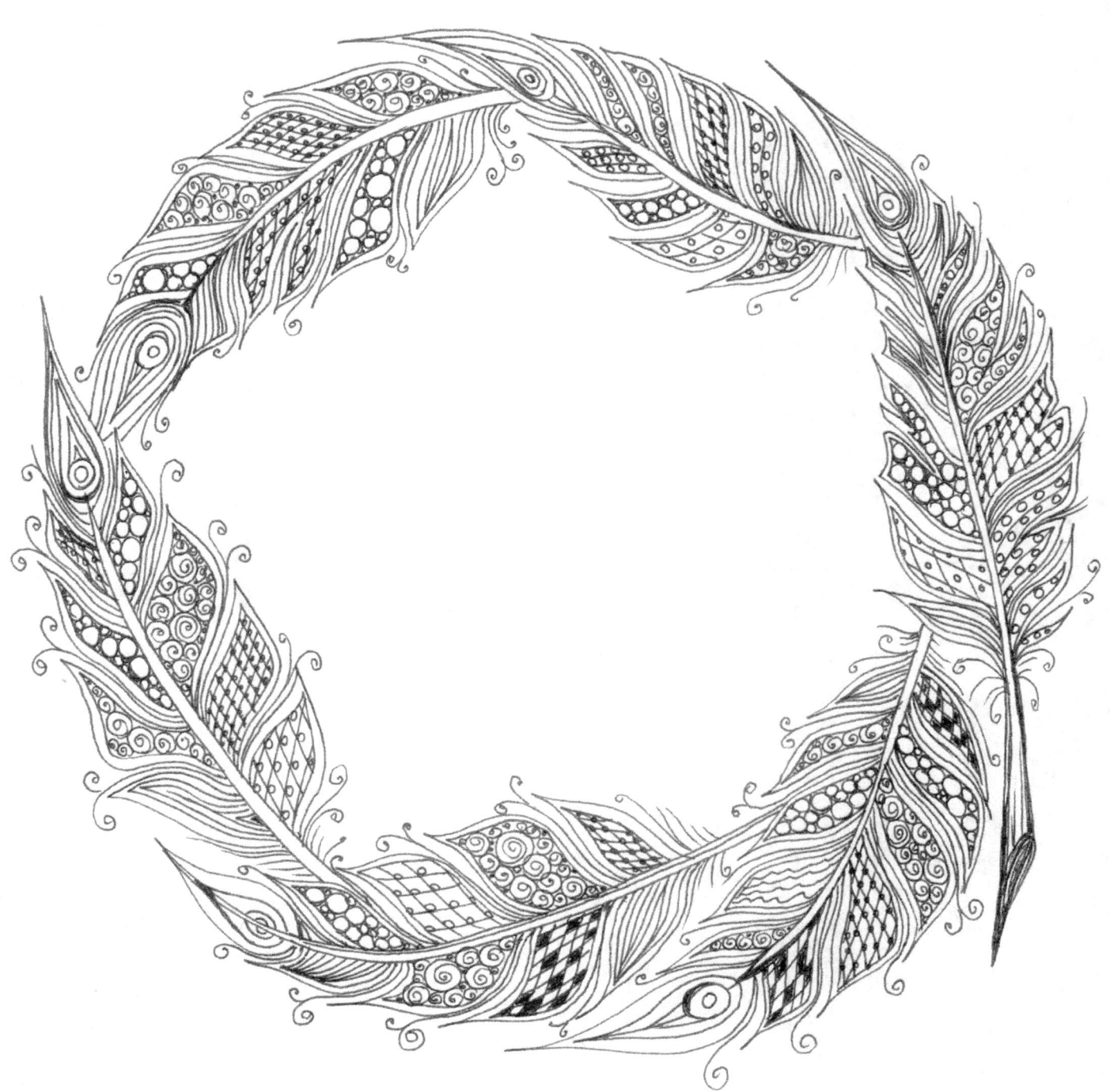

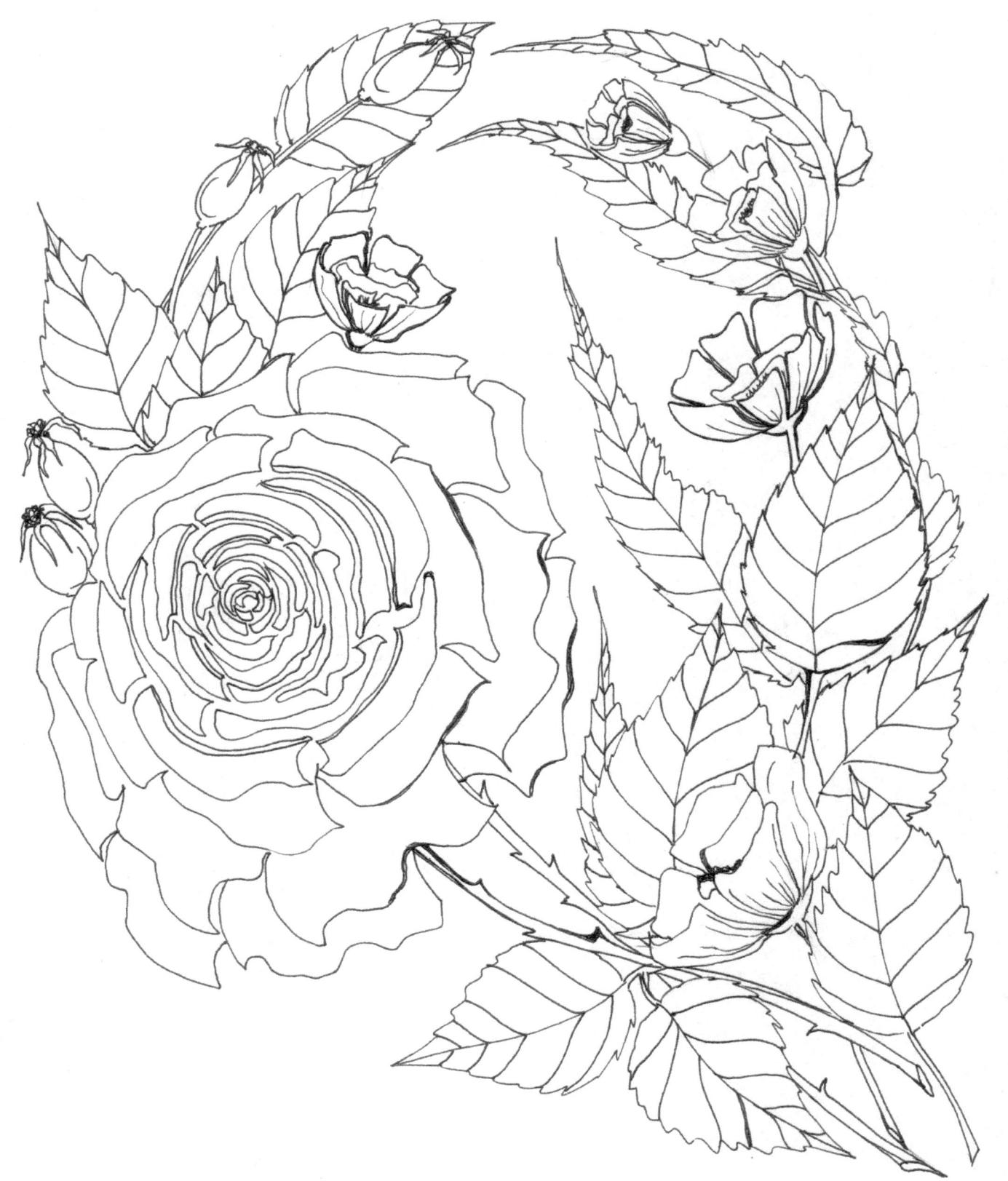

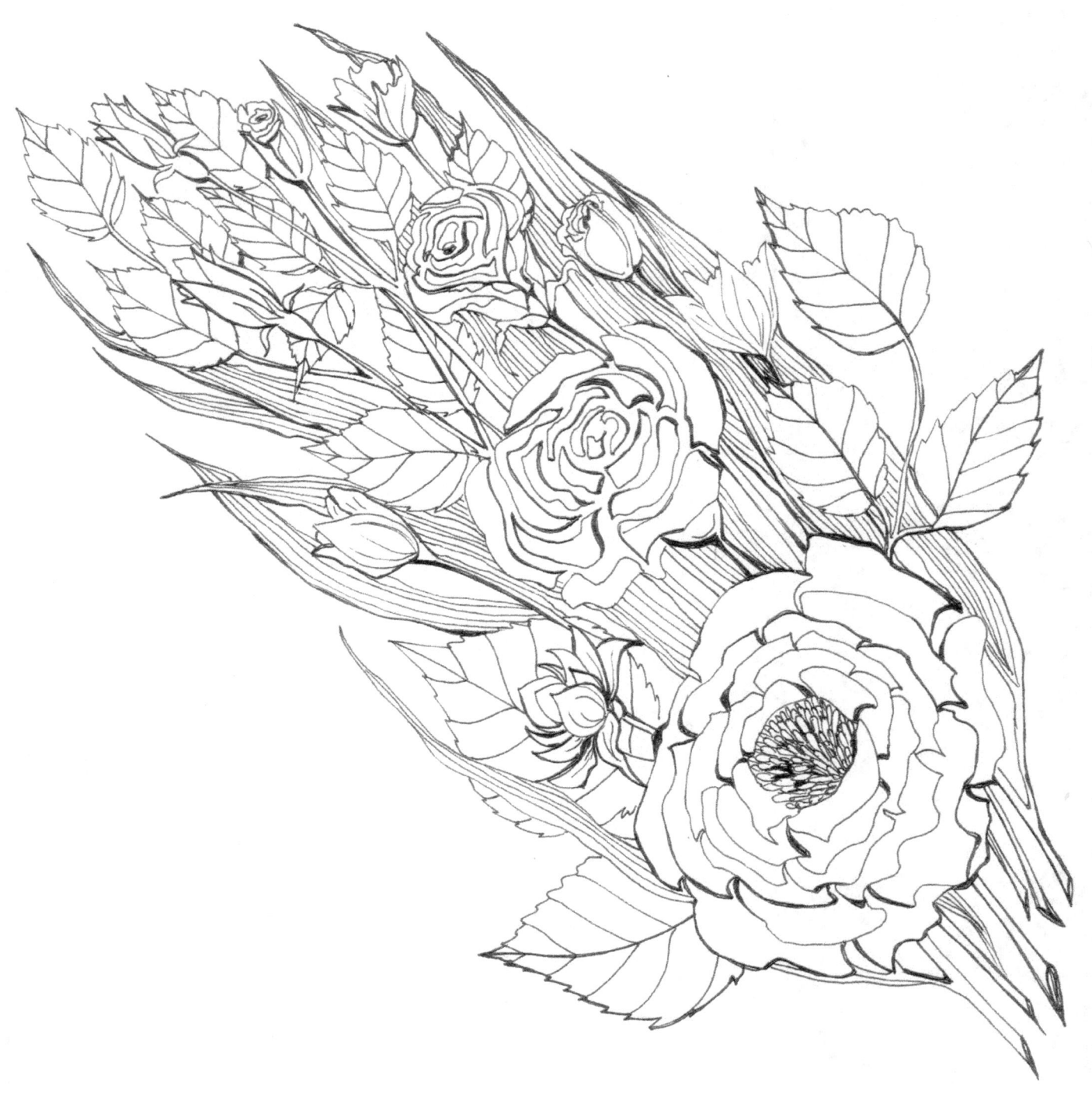

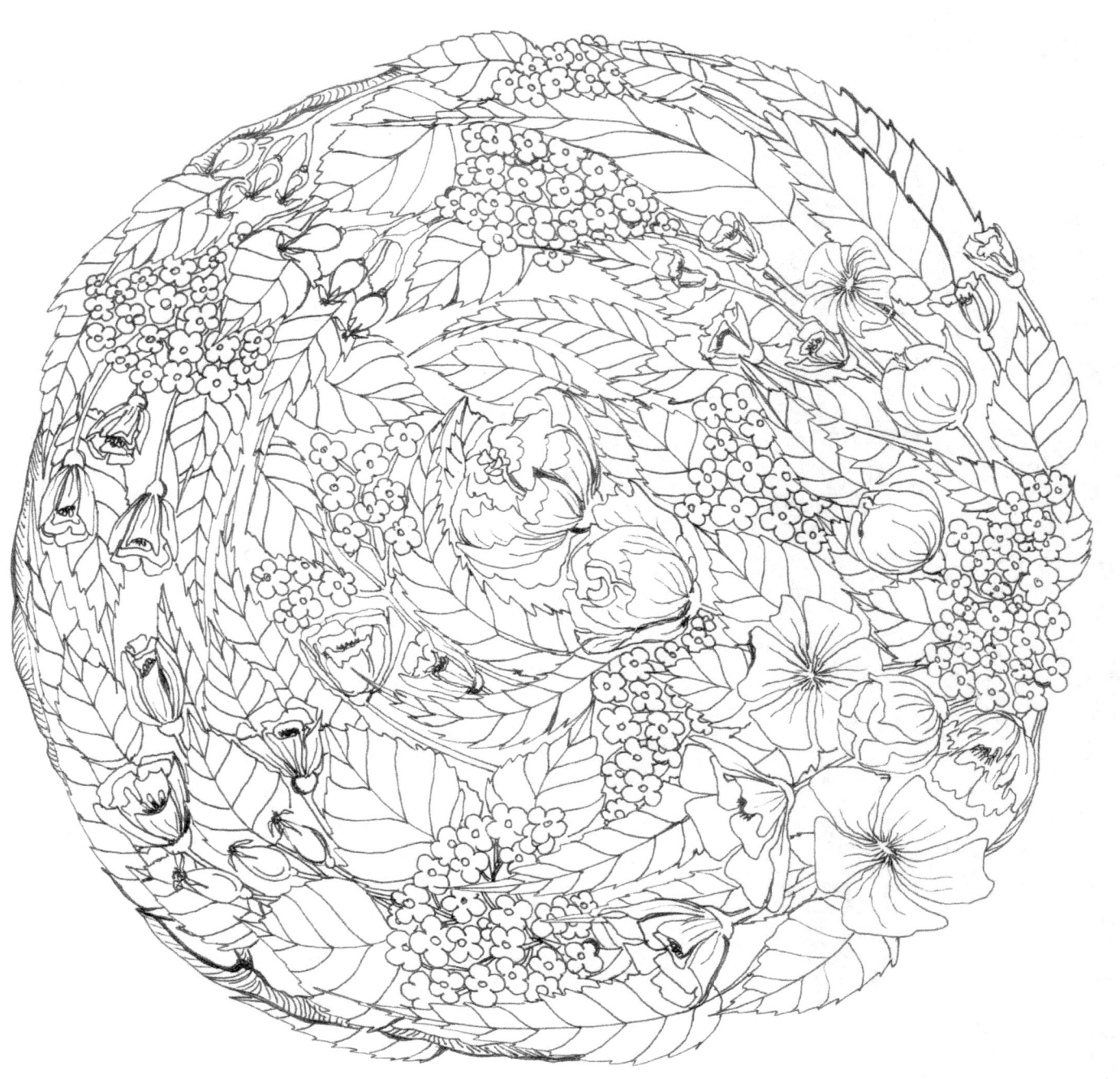

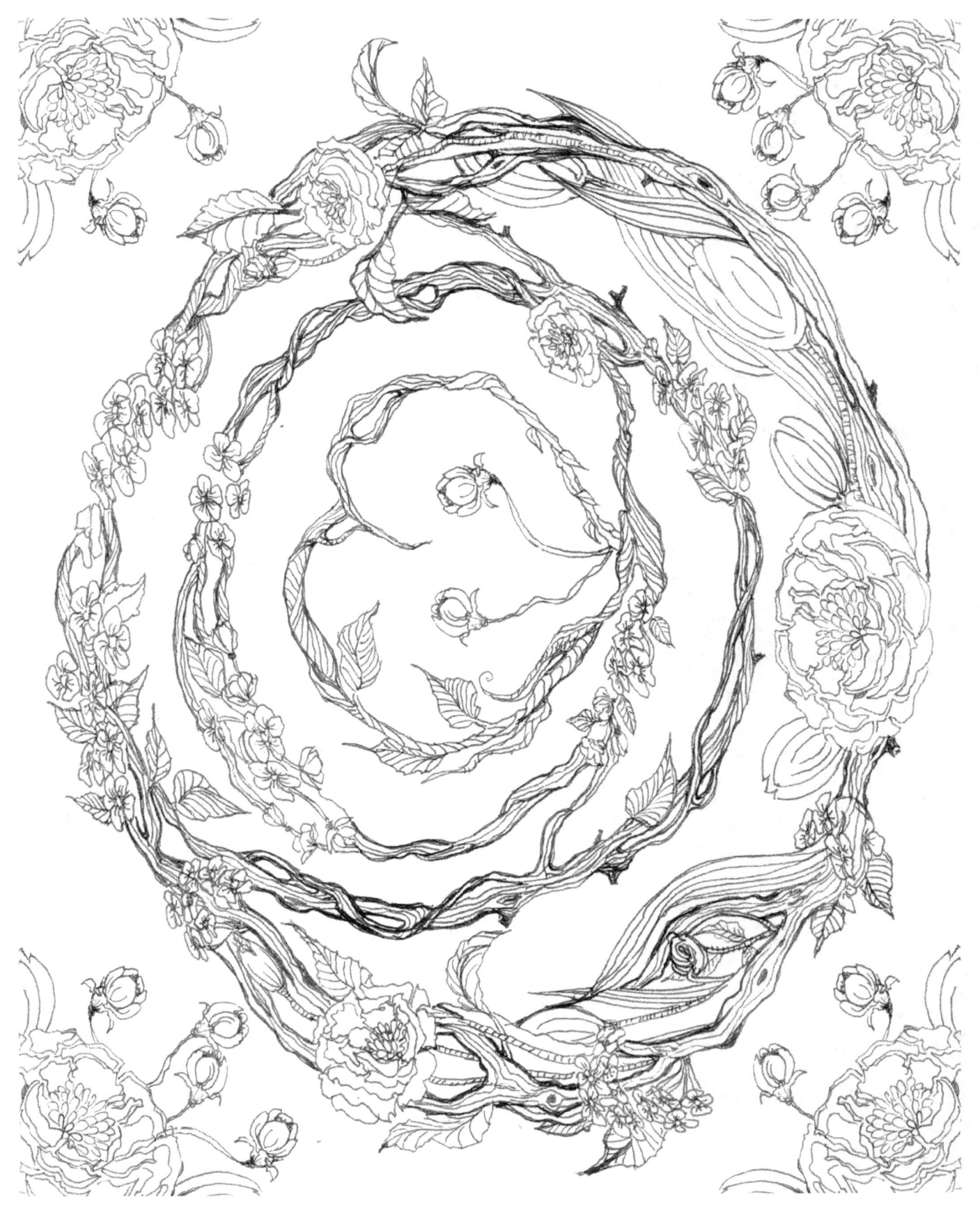

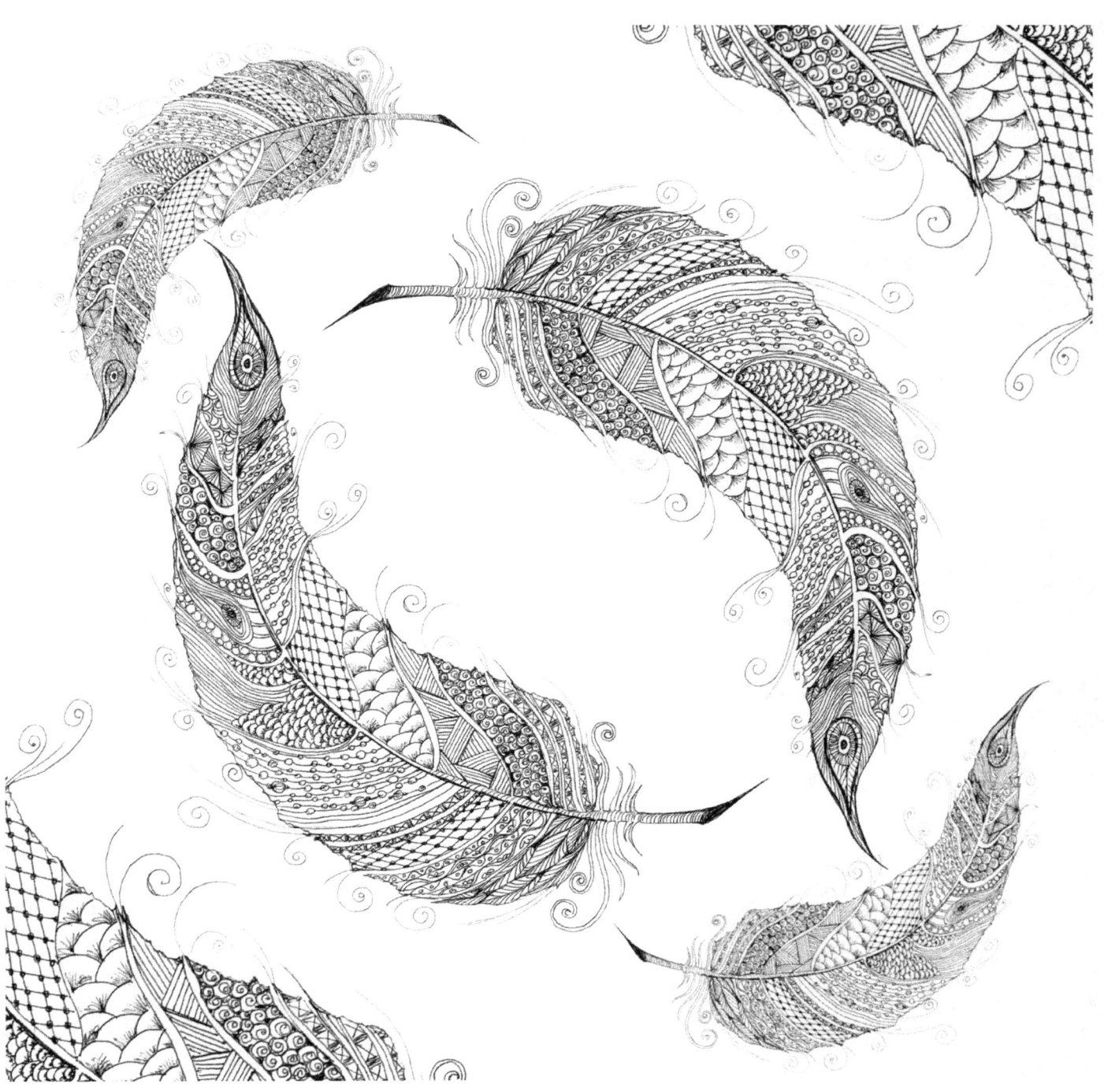

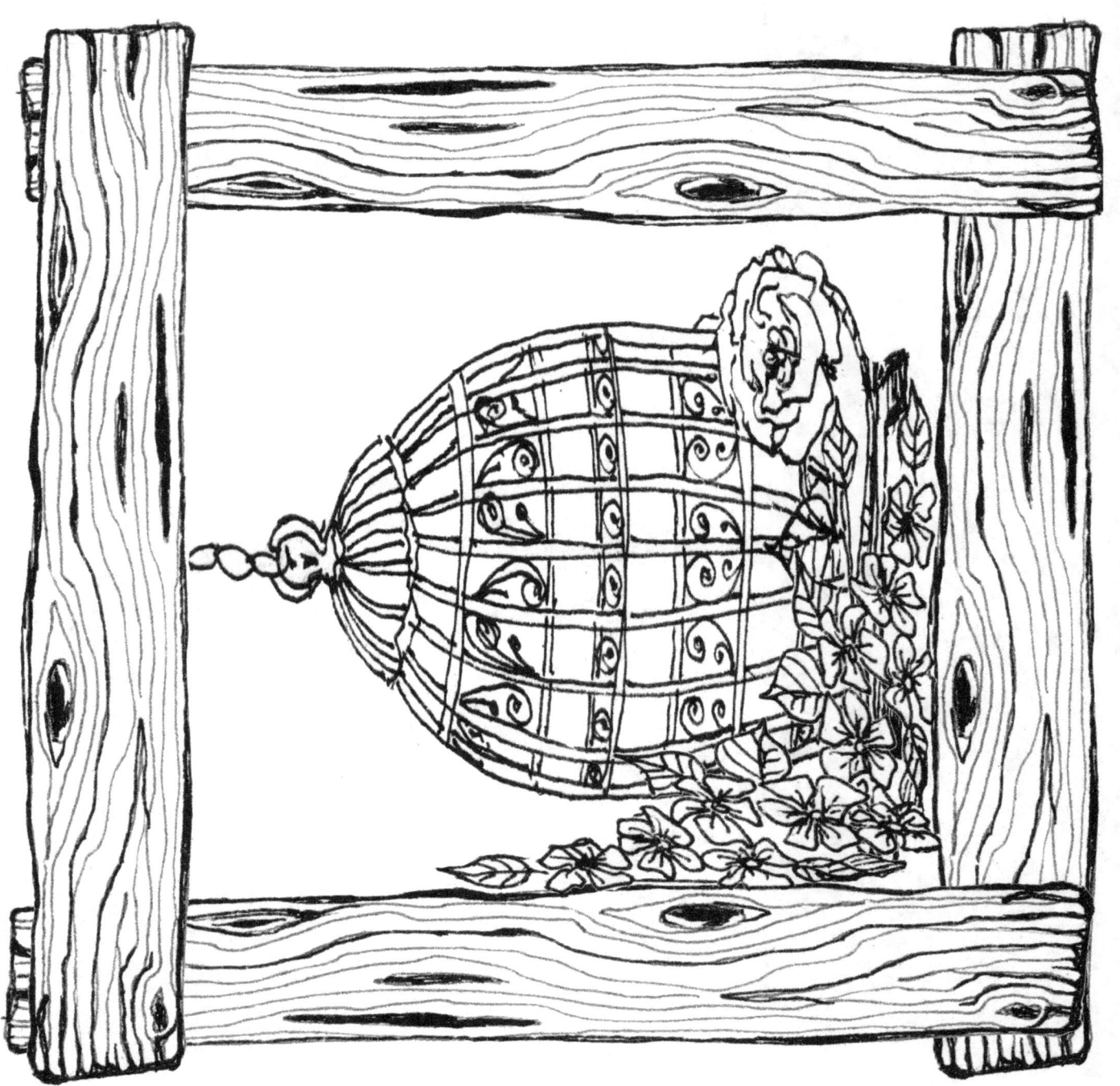

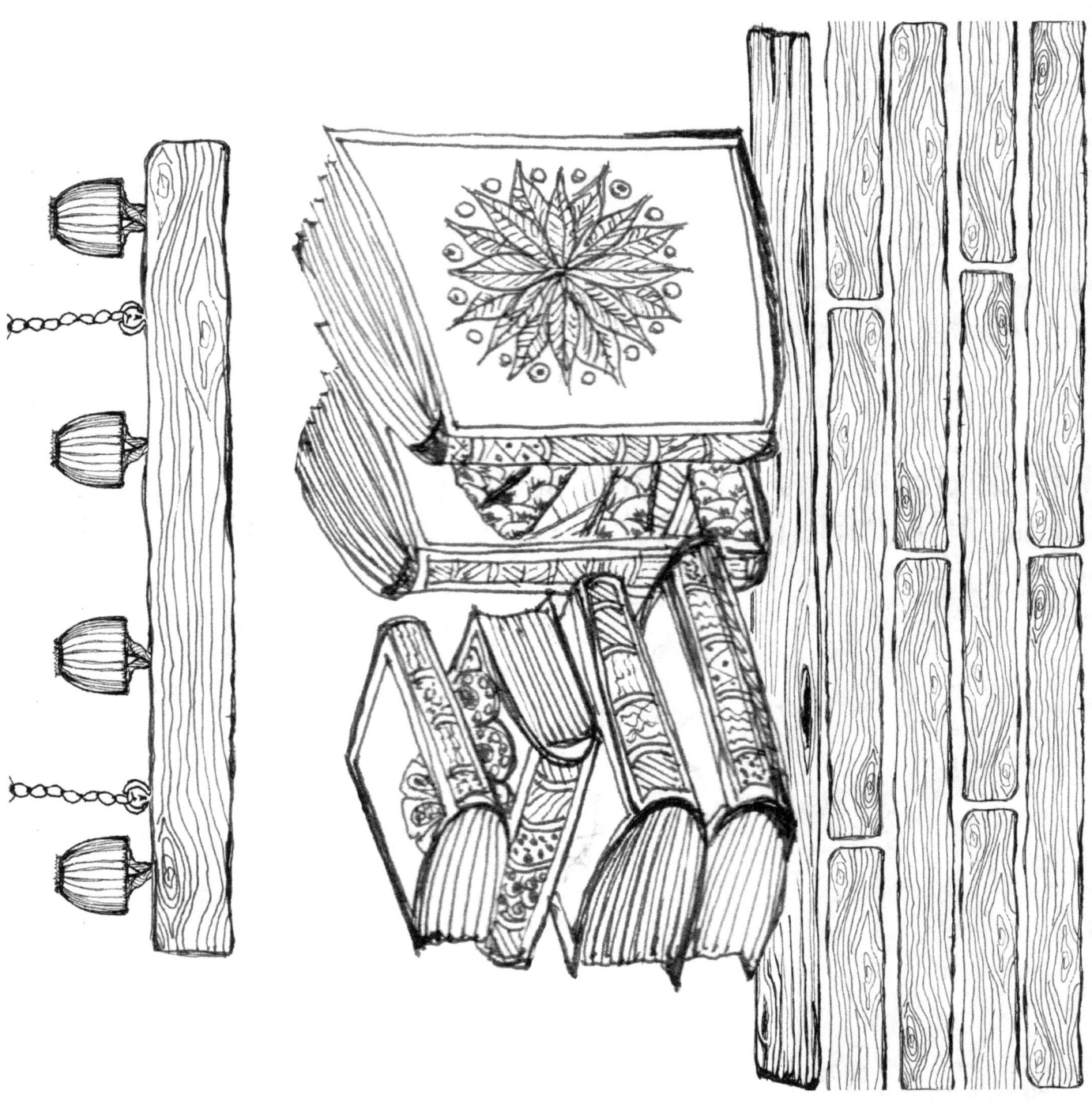

Paradoxically though it may seem, it is none the less true that life imitates art far more than art imitates life.

Oscar Wilde

ISBN-13: 978-1540698100
ISBN-10: 1540698106